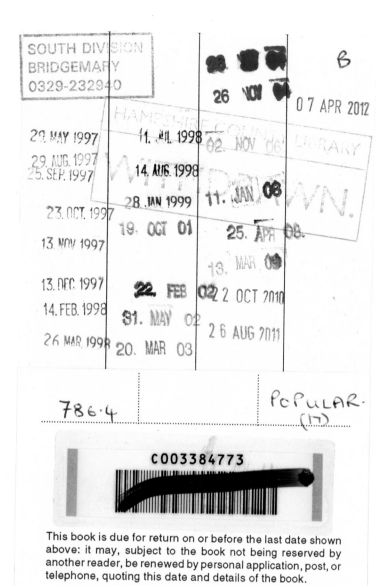

# POPULAR PIANO SOLOS · BOOK 17

SOA

WISE PUBLICATIONS
LONDON/NEW YORK/PARIS/SYDNEY/COPENHAGEN/MADRID

EXCLUSIVE DISTRIBUTORS:
MUSIC SALES LIMITED
8/9 FRITH STREET,
LONDON W1V 5TZ, ENGLAND.

MUSIC SALES PTY LIMITED
120 ROTHSCHILD AVENUE,
ROSEBERY, NSW 2018,
AUSTRALIA.

THIS BOOK © COPYRIGHT 1996 BY WISE PUBLICATIONS
ORDER NO. AM92084
ISBN 0-7119-4203-X

MUSIC ARRANGED BY STEPHEN DURO
MUSIC PROCESSED BY ALLEGRO REPRODUCTIONS
COMPILED BY PETER EVANS
ORIGINAL BOOK DESIGN BY HOWARD BROWN
COVER DESIGN BY PEARCE MARCHBANK, STUDIO TWENTY
MAIN PHOTOGRAPH COURTESY OF AKG LONDON

MUSIC SALES' COMPLETE CATALOGUE DESCRIBES THOUSANDS OF TITLES
AND IS AVAILABLE IN FULL COLOUR SECTIONS BY SUBJECT,
DIRECT FROM MUSIC SALES LIMITED.
PLEASE STATE YOUR AREAS OF INTEREST AND
SEND A CHEQUE/POSTAL ORDER FOR £1.50 FOR POSTAGE TO:
MUSIC SALES LIMITED, NEWMARKET ROAD,
BURY ST. EDMUNDS, SUFFOLK IP33 3YB.

PRINTED IN THE UNITED KINGDOM BY
REDWOOD BOOKS LIMITED, TROWBRIDGE, WILTSHIRE.

# A TASTE OF HONEY

WORDS BY RIC MARLOW
MUSIC BY BOBBY SCOTT

# COCKTAILS FOR TWO
WORDS & MUSIC BY ARTHUR JOHNSTON & SAM COSLOW

# COME FLY WITH ME

LYRICS BY SAMMY CAHN
MUSIC BY JAMES VAN HEUSEN

**Moderately with a beat**

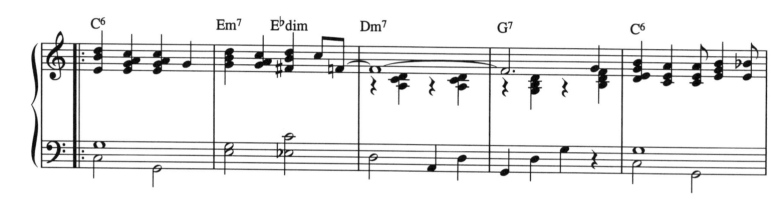

# GIRL TALK

WORDS & MUSIC BY NEAL HEFTI & BOBBY TROUP

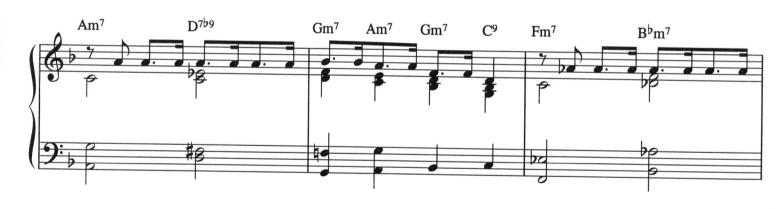

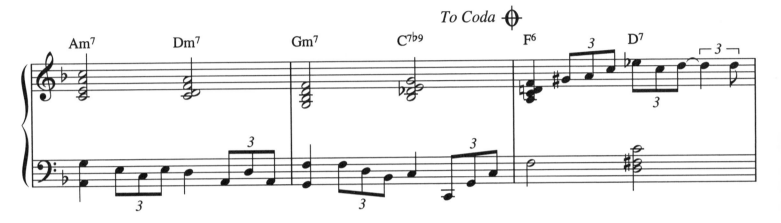

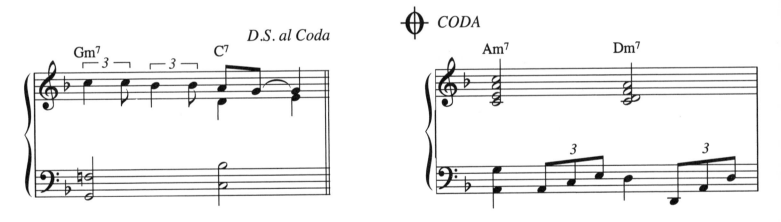

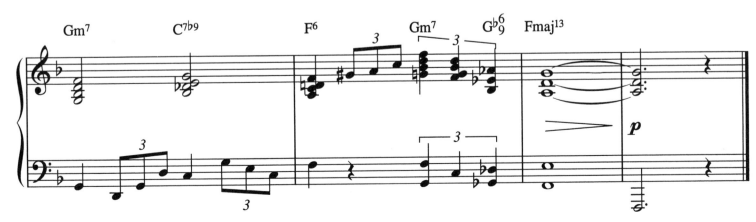

# HARLEM NOCTURNE

MUSIC BY EARLE HAGEN
WORDS BY DICK ROGERS

# HEART AND SOUL

MUSIC BY HOAGY CARMICHAEL
WORDS BY FRANK LOESSER

# HOW INSENSITIVE

MUSIC BY ANTONIO CARLOS JOBIM. ORIGINAL LYRICS BY
VINICIUS DE MORAES. ENGLISH LYRICS BY NORMAN GIMBEL

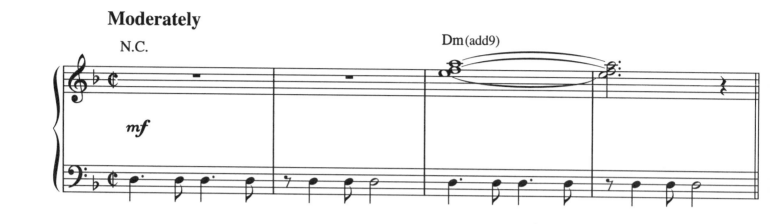

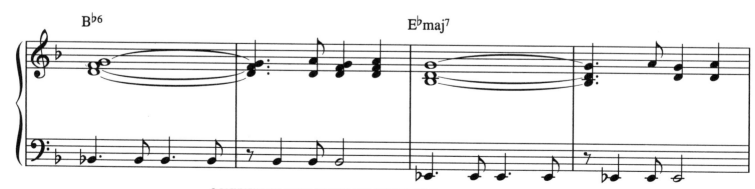

# I KNOW HIM SO WELL

WORDS & MUSIC BY BENNY ANDERSSON, TIM RICE & BJORN ULVAEUS

25

# ISN'T IT ROMANTIC

MUSIC BY RICHARD RODGERS
WORDS BY LORENZ HART

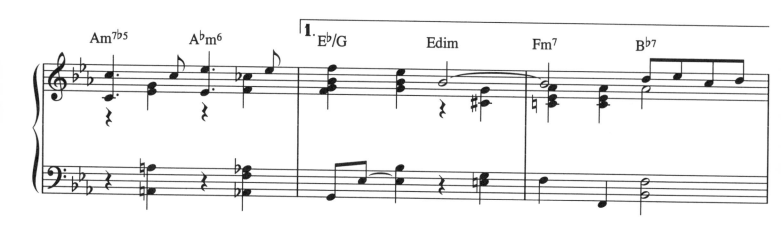

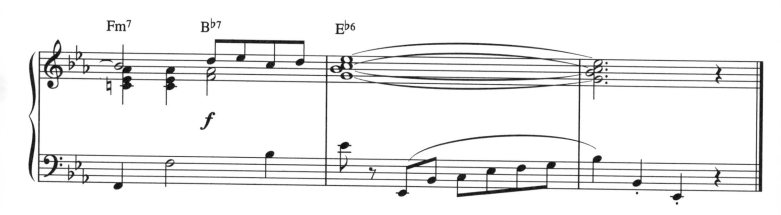

# IT AIN'T NECESSARILY SO (FROM 'PORGY AND BESS')

WORDS & MUSIC BY GEORGE GERSHWIN, DUBOSE & DOROTHY HEYWARD & IRA GERSHWIN

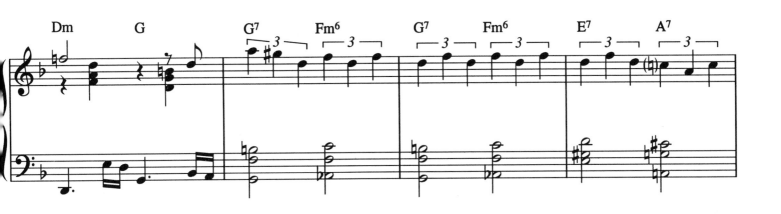

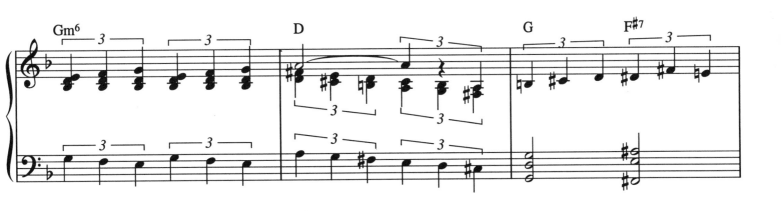

# LOVE LETTERS

MUSIC BY VICTOR YOUNG
WORDS BY EDWARD HEYMAN

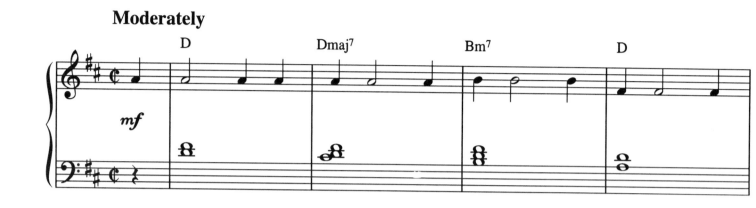

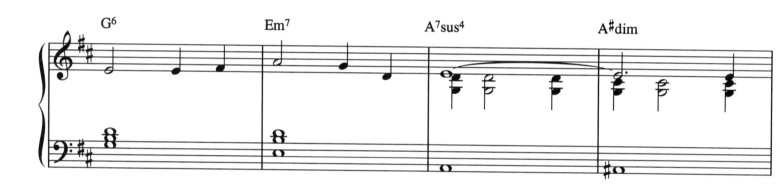

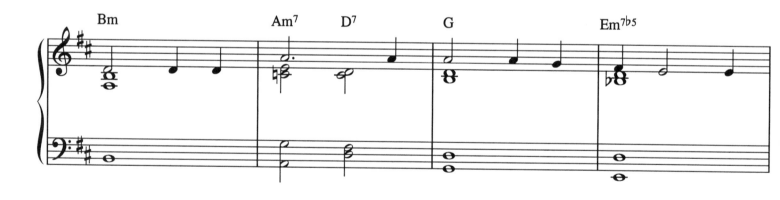

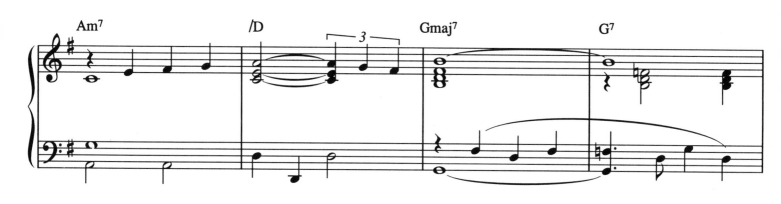

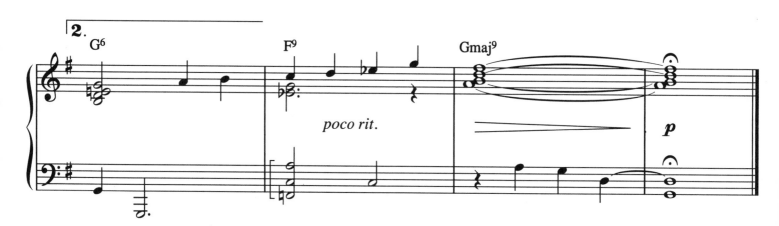

# MEDITATION (MEDITACAO)

ORIGINAL WORDS BY NEWTON MENDONCA. ENGLISH LYRIC BY NORMAN GIMBEL.
MUSIC BY ANTONIO CARLOS JOBIM

# MOON RIVER

MUSIC BY HENRY MANCINI
WORDS BY JOHNNY MERCER

**Moderately**

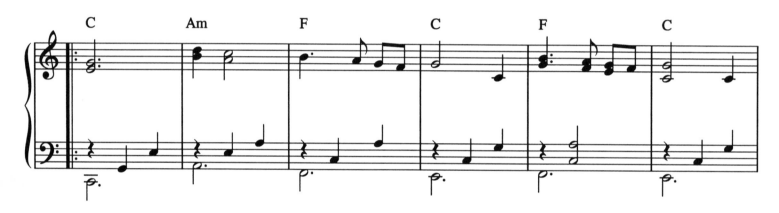

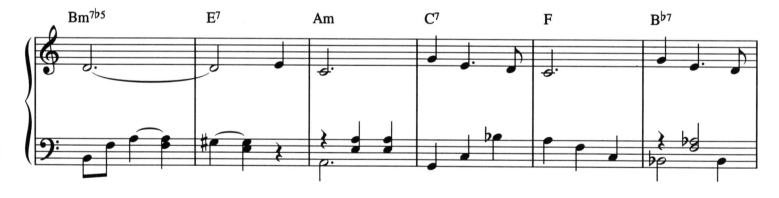

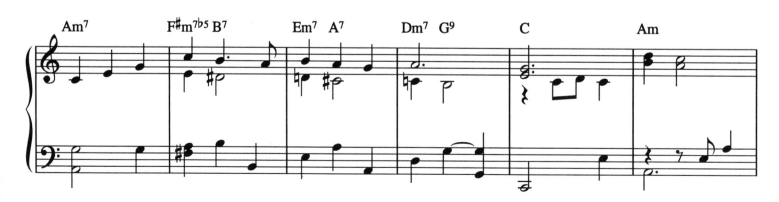

# STELLA BY STARLIGHT

MUSIC BY VICTOR YOUNG
WORDS BY NED WASHINGTON

# STRANGERS IN THE NIGHT

WORDS BY CHARLES SINGLETON & EDDIE SNYDER
MUSIC BY BERT KAEMPFERT

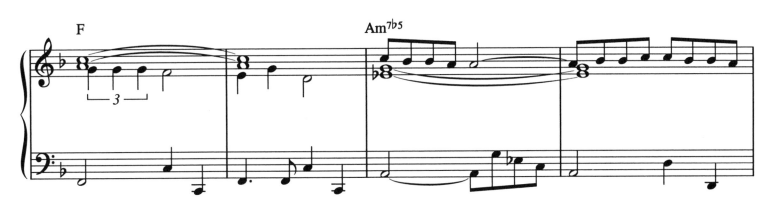

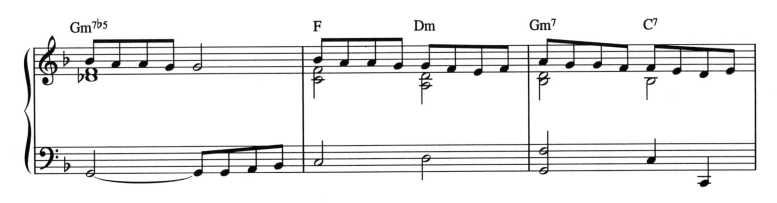

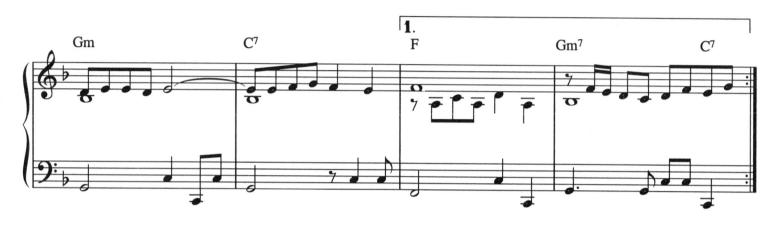

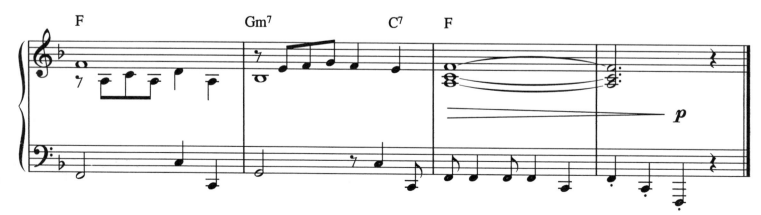

# Thanks For The Memory

WORDS & MUSIC BY LEO ROBIN & RALPH RAINGER

46

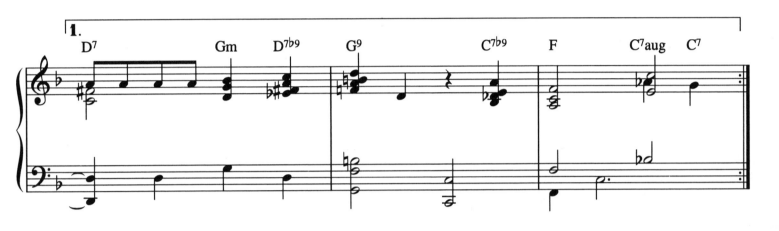

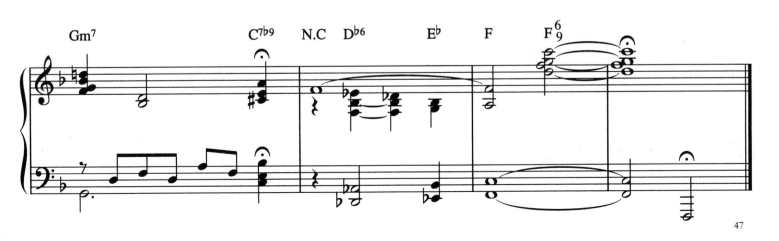

# THAT'S AMORE

WORDS & MUSIC BY JACK BROOKS & HARRY WARREN

**Moderately bright**

48

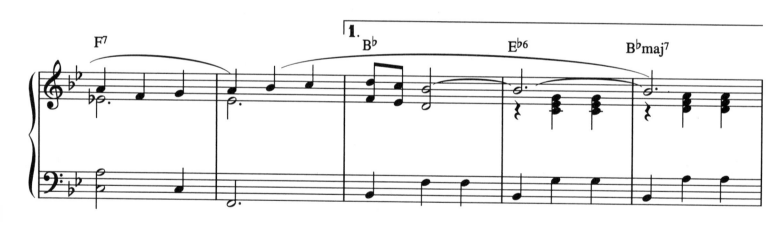

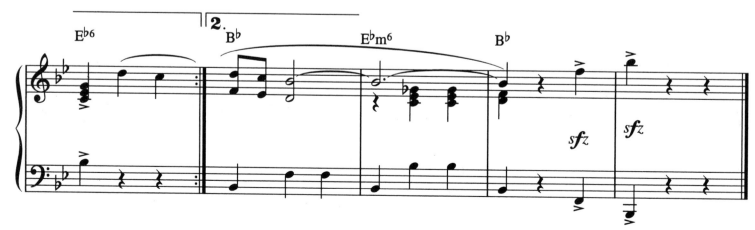

# THE TOUCH OF YOUR LIPS

WORDS & MUSIC BY RAY NOBLE

**Moderately**

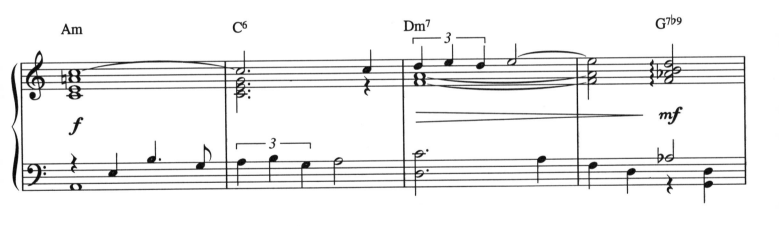

# UP WHERE WE BELONG

WORDS & MUSIC BY JACK NITZSCHE, WILL JENNINGS & BUFFY SAINTE MARIE

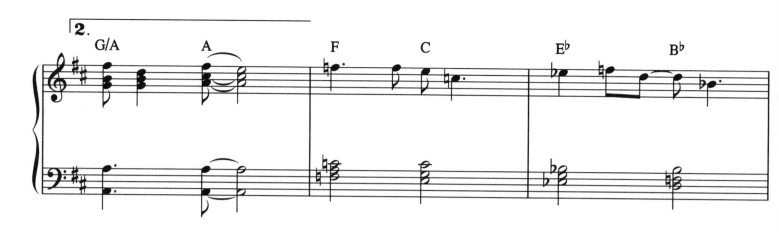

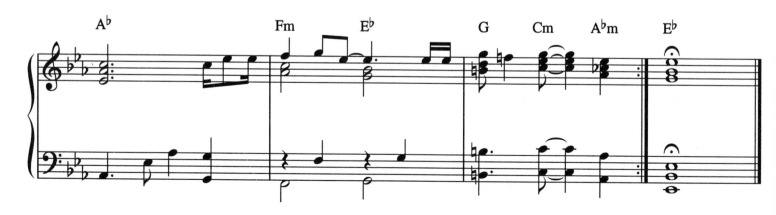

# WHERE DO I BEGIN (THEME FROM LOVE STORY)

MUSIC BY FRANCIS LAI
WORDS BY CARL SIGMAN

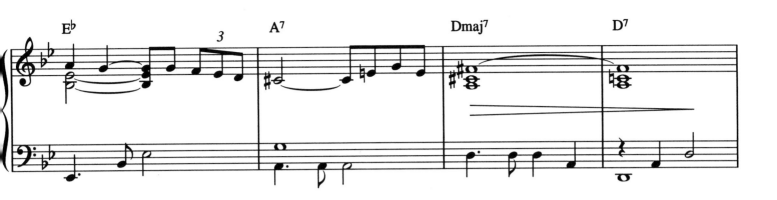

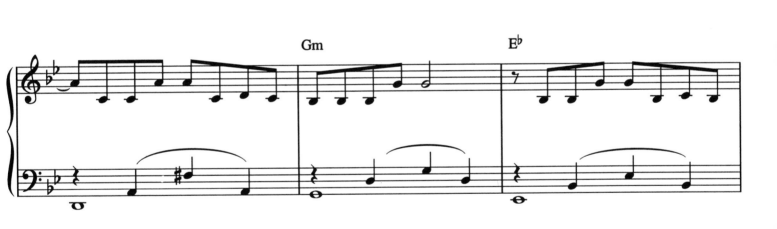

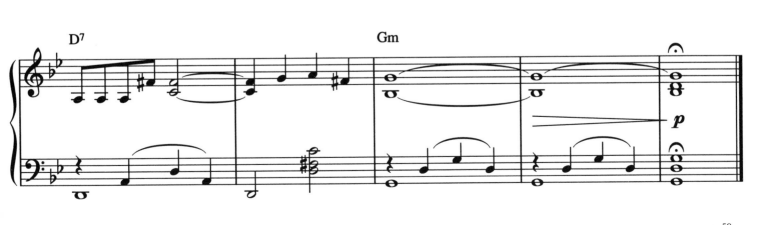

# WHEN I TAKE MY SUGAR TO TEA

WORDS & MUSIC BY IRVING KAHAL, SAMMY FAIN & PIERRE NORMAN CONNOR

# YOU BROUGHT A NEW KIND OF LOVE TO ME

WORDS & MUSIC BY SAMMY FAIN, IRVING KAHAL & PIERRE NORMAN CONNOR

**Moderately**

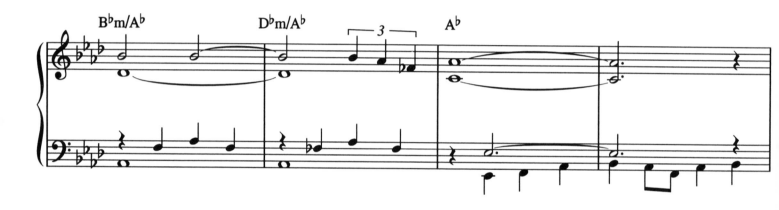

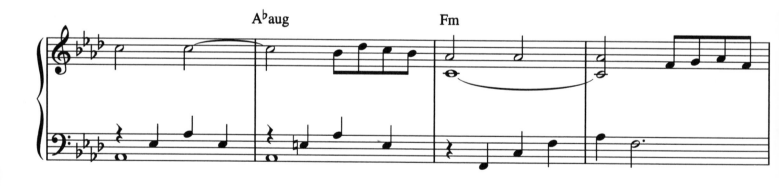

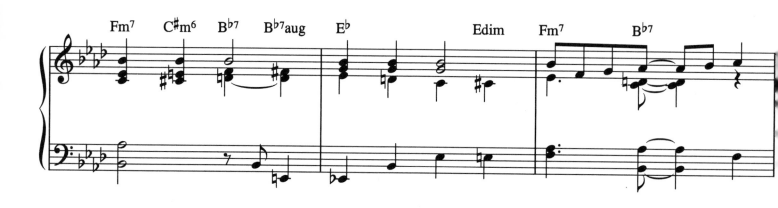